GUNS N' ROSES

The Photographic History

C000120950

The Photographic History

GUNS N' ROSES

PHOTOGRAPHS BY

ROBERT JOHN

Foreword by W. Axl Rose

Little, Brown and Company

Boston Toronto London

This book is dedicated to my mother, Louise John, and to the memory of my father, Robert C. John, and Todd Crew.

Frontispiece: Axl and Slash live at the Los Angeles Forum, 1991, on Guns N' Roses' first headline tour.

Copyright © 1993 by Robert John
Foreword © 1993 by W. Axl Rose

All rights reserved. No part of this book may be reproduced in any form or by any electronic or mechanical means, including information storage and retrieval systems, without permission in writing from the publisher, except by a reviewer who may quote brief passages in a review.

First Edition

Robert John's black-and-white photographs were printed by Alan's Custom Lab. Color photographs were printed by Chrome & "R."

Library of Congress Cataloguing-in-Publication Data
John, Robert, 1961—
    Guns N' Roses : the photographic history / Robert John ; foreword
by W. Axl Rose. — 1st ed.
        p.   cm.
    ISBN 0-316-46695-6 (pb)
    1. Guns N' Roses (Musical group) — Pictorial works. 2. Rock
musicians — United States — Pictorial works.   I. Title.
ML421.G86J6   1993
782.42166'092'2 — dc20
[B]   92-45731

10   9   8   7   6   5   4   3   2   1

RRD-OH

Designed by Barbara Werden

Published simultaneously in Canada by
Little, Brown & Company (Canada) Limited
Printed in the United States of America

F O R E W O R D

b y

W . A X L R O S E

Right now, at this particular point in my life, I'm a person who doesn't particularly like to have his fuckin' photograph taken. I grew tired of looking like I was competing to be the king of rock 'n' roll pinups. When I do a photo shoot, I get very ready for the photo shoot and I don't really want to do that anymore. I want to get to a place mentally where I can say, "Hey, this is me, capture it," and I'm not there yet. I'm trying to get myself healthy. I'd like to be captured on film when I've achieved that goal and not in between. Unless I'm onstage or doing something for a video, I'm not really into photos. I used to be and maybe that'll change. . . .

I think I met Robert John at the Troubadour. Izzy wanted him to shoot pictures of us in Rose, a band we had before Guns N' Roses. Robert was working with WASP at the time and Izzy was going out with the girl that WASP tied to the rack as part of their stage show. She eventually became Robert's girlfriend. Robert was just starting out, and when WASP got famous they didn't want to have anything to do with him. They dumped everybody they worked with. Izzy brought Robert around when we were putting Guns N' Roses together and we just hit it off right away. I took Robert's work real seriously because I saw his dedication towards it. Somehow, he and I hit it off and we've been friends ever since.

Robert used us to develop his skills, and that was cool because I wanted to see someone coming from the same place we were coming from developing our talents and growing together. Hollywood used to be like a smaller version of the big time, and club bands, ourselves included, would act like they were the world's biggest stars. Crazier decadence used to go on back then, and Robert was around for all of that. He grew with us through that period and always kept his head pretty together. He never got into ego battles with us and he never fucked us over. A lot of people did. We always wore what we wanted to wear or did what we wanted to do at the photo shoots, and Robert captured who we were rather than telling us to do something else.

My favorite photos of GN'R were the ones that no magazine would run. It was dark, abstract, moody ones. I like the darker aspects of GN'R, but magazines want pinup shots. That's a drag, but that's why this book exists. When we do shots together we carefully plan them out. I like that creative process. Other photographers have tried to capture that "GN'R Attitude" when they know absolutely nothing about what the GN'R attitude is. Robert's constantly been involved with Guns N' Roses since the beginning. He's really like the only photographer I trust. There might be other people who are technically better and more experienced, but no one shoots us better. Some people might think that anyone can shoot rock photography, but that's bullshit and prejudiced. No one's been more honest with us. Robert cares about us. I like and trust him as much as anyone in our organization. When we got signed to Geffen Records we were told we'd have to work with certain photographers. I said I wasn't going to sign the contract. Robert John comes with us and comes with us all the way. I'll say I'm going to shoot with someone else just to get everybody off my back, but I won't even show up. Why should we shoot with some magazine's photographer who we don't know or trust, who could be some hack mercenary out for himself, who doesn't care whether the shot is good or bad — and sometimes it appears that they prefer bad over good photos — when we know Robert will deliver? I hate parasitic photographers who don't care about the job they do, only about the money GN'R shots can bring in. A lot of photographers act like we're going to die tomorrow so they better get what they can now. They lose sight of the big picture. Robert has lost money in the past waiting for us to approve shots while other photographers made bucks spreading our photos around any- and everywhere they could.

We always, since the beginning, pressured Robert, especially when doing group shots. "All right, c'mon, let's get it over with." The group shot that we used in *Use Your Illusions* was a ten-minute session. That's the last group shot we've done. I haven't wanted to do a group shot in a very long time, and I haven't wanted to do any wild photos, like covering myself in blue paint or something, for a while now. When I do decide to do some shots Robert is the first person I'm gonna call.

Robert sticks by us and that's part of the reason we're loyal to him. Our relationship with Robert John has been one of our biggest problems with the press. We told magazines we wanted to use Robert. They said no, so we said, "All right then, we don't want to be in your magazine." We grew tired of being fucked around, so we stopped dealing with certain magazines. These magazines started running bootleg photographs, fake and made-up interviews, and then turned it around so we're the ones with the attitude problem. We don't allow cameras into our concerts, so if you pick up a magazine with a blurry live shot taken from the audience, that photographer and that magazine have no respect towards us and our wishes. And you're getting ripped by inferior product. We don't want the press and magazines to kiss our asses or anything, but we're helping them make money and our logic is, the better the photo, the more appealing the product. And Robert's photos of us are the best. Period.

Personally, when I see shots of hard rock artists that are phony, you know, in some macho pose that the camera conveniently captured, I feel let down. I'm never let down when I see intense live shots of Jane's Addiction, Sebastian Bach, or the Chili Peppers, because those bands are for real. When I perform I try to throw myself into the songs as hard as I can, and those are the shots you'll find in this book. Robert has a knack for knowing what's going on inside my head, and he knows when to shoot. How? I don't know, probably because he's been with us for so long that it's second nature to him. It looks more like action stills from a movie than a concert. We want the most intense moments, the most intense looks to be captured, and he does this better than anyone who's ever shot the band. He plans his shots that way instead of taking credit for a cool accident that happened, which is what a lot of photographers do when they shoot us. I like the way we're captured, and I'm glad that it's one of my closest friends doing that work.

Robert John is one of my best friends. He's a true friend in every aspect of the word. He's someone I can call at any time about anything and I can trust him with anything. He's always going to bat for me. When someone tries to get information about Guns N' Roses or me out of him, he's like, "No, sorry. That's personal." He's not an asshole about it. He's just trustworthy the way friends should be. And he doesn't take shit from anyone in the band, and that's cool too. He'll tell you exactly how he feels instead of brooding. I see Robert as a successful photographer taking pictures of what he wants to and enjoying it. I'm glad that one of the things he's chosen to take photos of is Guns N' Roses.

In actuality, Robert John is like a member of the band. Slash plays guitar and handles a lot of the business, Matt's job is being the drummer, Duff's is being the bassist. My job is frontman and being the pain in the ass that I am. Robert's like a member of the band whose job is photography. He's one of the fuckin' coolest people that I know, and whenever my back's been against the wall, Robert John is one of the first people here, and I really appreciate that. I know I can count on him and he knows he can count on me. And that's more important than the photos, Guns N' Roses, or whatever. If he needs help I'm gonna be there for him, and if I need help Robert is gonna be there for me. He's been there when I've been too pissed off about something and needed help cooling down. If anyone still doesn't know why we shoot with Robert John, the answer is character, that's why!

Since the early days, Robert and I talked about there being a Guns N' Roses photo book and people thought we were crazy. There are some photos in here that people are going to dig, and there are some photos of us that people are going to hate. The important thing is you are getting the entire Guns N' Roses photographic history as it went down. I hope people like it. Robert's been planning this book for quite a long time, and I'm very happy and proud to see him achieve his goal. Or at least one of them.

Sincerely,

W. Axl Rose
GN'R
92-

GUNS N' ROSES

The Photographic History

W. Axl Rose, raised in Lafayette, Indiana, came to Guns N' Roses after fronting bands called Rose and L.A. Guns.

Guns N' Roses at a construction site on the corner of Sunset and LaBrea, Hollywood, 1985. One of the band's first photo sessions. Left to right: Slash, W. Axl Rose, Steven Adler, Izzy Stradlin, Duff McKagan.

Slash, born in Stoke-on-Trent, England, but raised in Los Angeles. Came to Guns N' Roses to replace original guitarist Tracy Guns.

A shot for an early promotional flyer, 1985.

Izzy Stradlin, also from Lafayette, Indiana, was a childhood friend of Rose's who came to Los Angeles before him. He played guitar in a band called London before joining Guns N' Roses.

Izzy Stradlin live at the Country Club, Reseda, California, 1985. The Country Club was one of the more important clubs on the L.A. scene.

At the Country Club, 1985.

Duff McKagan, from Seattle, joined Guns N' Roses after responding to an ad for a bass player in a local music paper.

One of Guns N' Roses' first
publicity shots, from a
session in Steven Adler's
apartment.

Steven Adler, a schoolmate
chum of Slash's, joined
with Slash, replacing short-
time original drummer
Robert Gardner.

Slash at the Country Club, 1985.

In performance at the Country Club, 1985. Note Axl's seldom-seen derby.

Shot used for the "Move to the City" flyer, Hollywood, 1985.

Izzy, 1985.

Izzy and Axl in Izzy's
Hollywood apartment.

Axl, 1985.

Outside the infamous Gardner studio. This was a decadent little sweatbox where band members lived and rehearsed until they signed their record deal. Hollywood, 1986.

Duff and Izzy outside the
Gardner Studio.

Axl and Izzy live at the Whiskey Au Go-Go in Hollywood.
Guns N' Roses was one of the first bands to perform at
the Whiskey after it reopened in 1986.

Slash and Duff, California,
1985.

Slash live at the Troubadour, West Hollywood, 1986.
Guns N' Roses gained a lot of territory at the
Troubadour, going from opening act to headliners.

Guns during one of their
early club gigs at the
Troubadour, 1986.

Duff, Hollywood, 1986.

Duff live at the
Troubadour, 1986, in front
of an early Guns N' Roses
banner.

Axl live at the Roxy,
Hollywood, 1986. Guns N'
Roses was one of the few
L.A. bands that could sell
out both Friday and
Saturday nights at the
Roxy.

Guns N' Roses backstage
at UCLA after opening for
the Red Hot Chili Peppers,
Hollywood, 1986.

Axl and Duff at rehearsal.

Axl and Duff on the front
cover of the *Live Like a
Suicide* EP. The shot was
taken live at the
Troubadour, 1986.

Axl live at the Troubadour,
1986.

Axl with Paul Stanley of
Kiss at Raji's on Hollywood
Boulevard. Stanley was
interested in producing
Guns N' Roses, but the
band passed.

Slash in the alley after a
Guns N' Roses performance
at Raji's, 1986.

Slash after a show at the
Roxy, Hollywood, 1986.

Axl live at the Roxy.

Axl, Los Angeles, 1986.

Guns N' Roses at a gas
station on the corner of
LaBrea and Romaine,
1986.

Out in the L.A. night,
1986. Geffen Records used
this as a publicity still
after signing Guns N' Roses
in 1986.

Steven Adler live at the
Roxy.

Axl fucking around in his
bathtub, 1987.

During the recording of
Appetite for Destruction at
Take One Studio, Burbank,
California, 1987.

Slash and Duff in some
dead guy's trash,
Hollywood, 1987.

Duff on a pool table at
Fenders, Long Beach,
California, 1987.

Overleaf:
Outtake shot for the single
"Welcome to the Jungle."

Hollywood, 1987.

Slash and Duff in discussion during preproduction of
Appetite for Destruction, Take One Studio, 1987.

Duff catching up on his
reading at Rumbo Studio.

Izzy taking a break during
the recording of *Appetite
for Destruction*.

Izzy on the roof of a hotel
after an all-nighter in
Atlanta on the Mötley Crüe
tour, 1987.

Duff and ex-JetBoy bassist Todd Crew jamming in their
side project, The Drunk Fux, at the Coconut Teaser,
Hollywood. Todd, a close friend of the band's, passed
away in 1987. He's greatly missed.

Izzy, Axl, and Slash live at
Fenders, Long Beach,
California, 1987.

Live in England, 1987.

Axl with a case of spotted
dick, England, 1987.

Slash and Duff in a London
hotel that the band would
eventually be banned
from, 1987.

Slash and Duff on the
streets of London.

Axl during the recording of
Appetite for Destruction, 1987.

Slash in the Take One Studio parking lot with Guns N'
Roses' rented van, 1987.

Izzy crashed in his hotel
room, Toronto, Canada,
1987.

Izzy live at the Marquee
Club, Soho, 1987.

Steven at Take One Studio,
1987.

A publicity still for *Appetite for Destruction.*

Outtake for the back cover
of *Appetite for Destruction*,
1987.

Axl with Erin Everly
backstage at the Celebrity
Theatre in Anaheim,
California, 1988. They
were married and divorced
in 1990.

Axl hamming it up in the dining room of his Hollywood apartment on Sycamore and 3rd, 1988.

Duff in the Hollywood Boulevard apartment that he shared with *RIP* writer Del James, 1988.

In front of a banner flying the Guns N' Roses logo: Steven Adler, Slash, Axl Rose, Izzy Stradlin, Duff McKagan. This shot was taken at six in the morning, after fifteen hours of filming the "Sweet Child o' Mine" video. Los Angeles, 1988.

Axl live at the Texas Jam.
Guns N' Roses appeared
with Iggy Pop, Ziggy
Marley, and INXS, 1988.

Slash flying on the
Aerosmith tour, 1988. This
was the band's most
important tour to date.

What's a shower without a
smoke? Slash, 1988.

Axl in leathers, 1988.

Duff, Nikki Sixx of Mötley
Crüe, and Slash backstage
during the Guns N' Roses/
Mötley Crüe Tour, Atlanta,
1988.

Steven Adler backstage at the Los Angeles Coliseum when
Guns N' Roses opened for the Rolling Stones.

Outtake from the *Rolling Stone* shoot through the broken
mirror in the living room of Axl's condominium, 1989.

Axl in his West Hollywood condominium. This photo was used on the front cover of the August 10, 1989, issue of *Rolling Stone.*

Slash in an abandoned car.

Slash live at the Park
Plaza, Los Angeles, at *RIP*
magazine's third annual
party, 1989.

Duff onstage with his trombone-playing brother, Matt
McKagan, at the Los Angeles Coliseum when Guns N'
Roses opened for the Rolling Stones, 1989.

Slash live at the Los Angeles Coliseum.

Duff with his mountain bike in Studio City, California.

Outtake from a photo session for the cover of *Car Audio* magazine, 1990.

Duff on Mulholland Drive
near his house in the
Hollywood Hills.

Overleaf:

Slash, Duff, Axl, Sebastian Bach from Skid Row, and Lars
Ulrich from Metallica, backstage at the *RIP* magazine's
fourth annual party, where the three bands jammed
together and discussed the possibility of doing a
monstrous tour someday. Hollywood Palladium, 1990.

Axl at home, 1989.

Slash at home, May 1989.

Axl during the recording of *Use Your Illusion* I & II at the
Record Plant in Hollywood, 1990. Axl would eventually
set up camp and move into the studio.

Izzy live during the "Get
in the Ring" Tour,
Washington, D.C., 1991.
Their first arena tour as
headliners, it opened at
the Alpine Valley Music
Theater in Wisconsin, May
24, 1991.

Slash with one of the
snakes from his collection,
1989.

Matt Sorum before his first show as drummer for Guns N'
Roses. Sorum, formerly with the Cult, replaced Steven
Adler. "Rock in Rio II," Rio De Janeiro, Brazil, 1991.

Slash in front of the Natural History Museum, London.

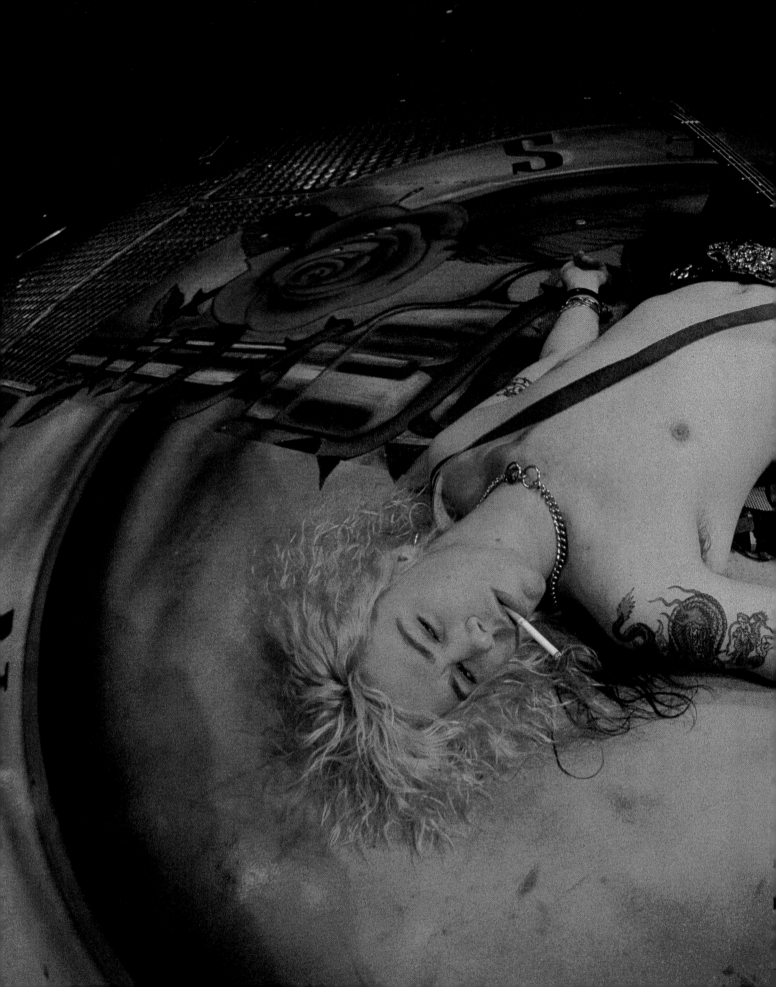

Duff on the Guns N' Roses
logo during rehearsals for
the "Get in the Ring" tour.

Keyboardist Dizzy Reed live. Dizzy, formerly with the L.A. club band The Wild, joined Guns N' Roses right before the band recorded *Use Your Illusion* I & II.

Axl live at the Warfield Theatre, San Francisco, during a warm-up gig for the "Get in the Ring" tour. A wild beginning for a wild tour.

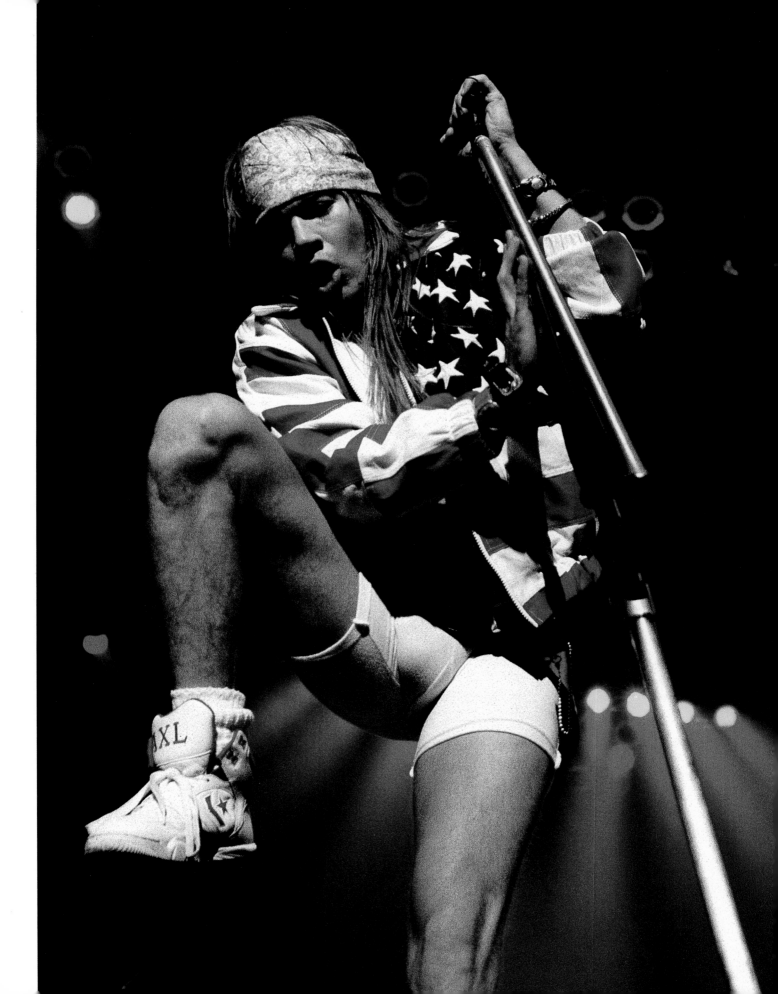

Slash en route to São Paulo, Brazil, to see rare snakes.

Duff, Slash, and Izzy live at the Los Angeles Forum, Inglewood, California, 1991. Guns N' Roses sold out four nights on their home turf.

Overleaf:
Axl and Slash live at the Los Angeles Forum.

Axl and Slash live in
Colorado, 1991.

Axl live at the Tokyo
Dome, 1991.

Axl in his new Honda Pilot,
1991.

Slash backstage during
the filming of MTV's
Tenth Anniversary
Special.

Slash live at the Tokyo
Dome, 1991.

Overleaf:
Slash and Duff at the Los Angeles Forum on the fourth
and final sold-out night. The band played for more than
three and a half hours, and the show was voted 1991
Gig of the Year by *RIP* magazine.

Duff live in Japan.

Slash live at Madison
Square Garden.

Axl live at the Warfield
Theater, San Francisco,
1991. Dumpster opened
for Guns N' Roses.

Slash vs. sunlight, Toronto,
Canada, 1991.

Slash live, Frankfurt,
Germany, 1991.

Axl during the filming of
the "Don't Cry" video, Los
Angeles, 1991.

Axl and Stephanie Seymour
having a picnic in a
cemetery during the
"Don't Cry" video shoot.

San Francisco, 1991.

Slash and Axl live in
Florida, 1991.

Axl flying through the air at the Ritz during the filming of the video for "You Could Be Mine." Axl wound up hurting his left heel and started the "Get in the Ring" tour in a special cast. New York City, 1991.

Guns N' Roses onstage,
Mannheim, Germany.

Duff in the crowd after
stage diving.

Duff, Guns N' Roses
manager Doug Goldstein,
and Slash taking care of
bidnis. Somewhere over
America, 1991.

Izzy relaxing during sound
check, Brazil, 1991.

Live at the Ritz, New York City. The back of the T-shirts for these warm-up shows declared, "Here Today, Gone To Hell." Raging Slab opened for Guns N' Roses.

Matt, Slash, and Duff in a
dressing room.

Matt live, Los Angeles
Forum, August 1991.

Slash onstage with Michael Jackson at MTV's Tenth
Anniversary Special, Los Angeles, 1991.

Slash live, Guns N' Roses
headline tour, 1991.

Slash and Izzy live, Los
Angeles Forum, 1991.

Axl live in Colorado, 1991.

Axl at Madison Square
Garden, December 1991.
The Thursday night show,
best of the band's three-
night stand.

Outtake from the group session for *Use Your Illusion* I & II.

Guitarist Gilby Clark joins Guns N' Roses after Izzy
Stradlin quits, 1991. Gilby came by way of Kill for Thrills
and the L.A. club band Blackouts.

Gilby in a limousine in
Tokyo, 1991.

Duff signing autographs in
Japan.

Gilby live, Europe somewhere.

Slash live at the Tokyo Dome, 1991.

Duff before the release of *Use Your Illusion*.

Dizzy during the sound check at Joe Robbie Stadium,
Miami, New Year's Eve 1991.

Slash with Renee Suran,
backstage, Washington,
D.C. They were married in
1992.

Slash live in Turin, Italy,
1992.

Overleaf:
Axl in front of 115,000
fans during "Rock in Rio
II," 1991.

Dizzy and Gilby in New
York City, 1992.

Matt in Ireland with a
local dog, May 1992.

Slash jumping during a sound check at International
Raceway, Phoenix. Guns N' Roses co-headlined this
stadium tour with Metallica. Faith No More opened the
show.

Axl live, looking mean in
his Mean Machine football
jersey.

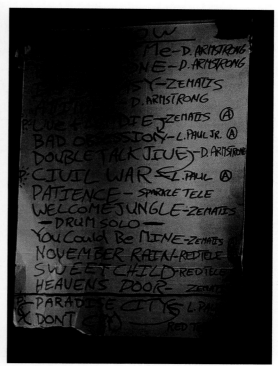

Song list, Phoenix, August
1992.

View of Jack Murphy
Stadium, San Diego, from
a helicopter during
intermission between
Metallica and Guns N'
Roses. Body Count opened
the show.

Dizzy live in Hanover,
Germany, June 1992.

Axl onstage, during a
moment of deep thought.

Gilby photographs the
photographer, MTV
Awards, 1992.

Slash with pyros, Columbia,
South Carolina, September
1992.

Gilby and Slash, December 1991.

Slash showing off.

Axl being mobbed by the audience at the Tacoma
(Washington) Dome after stage diving, July 17, 1991.

Slash with Aerosmith's Steven Tyler right before the Guns
N' Roses Pay-Per-View show broadcast live from Paris.
Soundgarden opened the show.

Matt live, Seattle, 1992.

Duff onstage in his
hometown, Seattle,
October 1992.

Axl, Duff, and Gilby on the
MGM Grand, 1992.

Duff, Slash, and Matt
arriving in Germany after
a long flight on the *MGM
Grand*, 1992.

Axl hanging out under the
band's plane, 1992.

Slash in a hotel jacuzzi,
Los Angeles, 1992.

Gilby, from a photo
session for *Guitar World*,
1992.

Duff live in Rotterdam,
Holland, June 1992.

Slash, Della Alpi Stadium,
Turin, Italy, 1992.

Axl in his hometown of
Lafayette, Indiana, July 23,
1992. The trees in the
background were planted
by Axl, his brother Stuart,
and his sister Amy.

Slash hanging out in a
cemetery in Brompton,
England, June 1992.

Slash waiting for a plane,
somewhere on tour in
Europe, 1992.

Axl talking with U2's Bono, backstage at the Mungerdorferstadion in Cologne, Germany, May 1992. Axl is a big U2 fan.

Duff and Axl, live in
Manchester, England, June
1992.

Slash during the last show of the Guns N' Roses/Metallica
summer stadium tour, Seattle, 1992.

Axl and Duff at the Silver
Dome, Pontiac, Michigan,
1992.

Axl during the making of "November Rain," New Mexico, 1992.

Slash, from a shoot for *Guitar World*, 1992.

Axl takes a breather
during the show, Santiago,
Chile, 1992.

Duff, Slash, and Axl live,
1992.

Overleaf:
Slash, Gilby, and Axl live during "Paradise City," Giants
Stadium, New Jersey, July 1992.

Duff with new bride, Linda
Johnson, 1992.

Axl live.

End of the show.

ACKNOWLEDGMENTS

Special thanks to Guns N' Roses: Axl, Slash, Duff, Matt, Gilby, and Dizzy; Izzy Stradlin; Doug Goldstein (for his support and friendship); Bryn ("Film is cheap in the long run") Bridenthal; Del James (for inspiring me to do this book and for the captions); Chanyn Coffin (for rocking my world); Neil Zlowzower (for all the help over the years); Tony Gardner (for making this book happen); Lonn Friend (for publishing photos no one else would dare to); Grant Chamberlain (for introducing me to photography); Gene Kirkland; and Michael Pietsch.

Thanks also to Tom Zutaut, Mike Clink, Michael Rotundo, Dave Drucker at Verdugo Hills Contact Lens, Mark Canter, Marty Temme, Kevin Walsh, Michael Golob, Denise Cox, Lori Earl, Brian Lysaght, Larry Carny at Samys Camera, Chris and Jim at Pix Camera, Tony Pashalides at Chrome & "R," Alan Wedertz at Alan's Custom Lab, everybody at A & I Color Lab, Wendy Schaffer, Riki Rachtman, Wendy Laister, Ross Halfin, Sofie Howard, Terrie Berg, Rick Castillo, Billy White, Chris Jones, Tom Maher, John Reese, and everybody on the Guns N' Roses crew.

Robert John
Photo by Gene Kirkland